Life Through Poetry

Edited by Sarah Marshall

First published in Great Britain in 2005 by:
Poetry Now
Remus House
Coltsfoot Drive
Peterborough
PE2 9JX
Telephone: 01733 898101
Website: www.forwardpress.co.uk

SB ISBN 1 84602 014 X

Foreword

Although we are a nation of poets we are accused of not reading poetry, or buying poetry books. After many years of listening to the incessant gripes of poetry publishers, I can only assume that the books they publish, in general, are books that most people do not want to read.

Poetry should not be obscure, introverted, and as cryptic as a crossword puzzle: it is the poet's duty to reach out and embrace the world.

The world owes the poet nothing and we should not be expected to dig and delve into a rambling discourse searching for some inner meaning.

The reason we write poetry (and almost all of us do) is because we want to communicate: an ideal; an idea; or a specific feeling. Poetry is as essential in communication, as a letter; a radio; a telephone, and the main criterion for selecting the poems in this anthology is very simple: they communicate.

Contents

The Poems

Haikus

Yellow buds peep through
The birds are singing sweetly
Morning has broken.

Humming bees gather
Blossoms release sweet nectar
Soft and fragrant dew.

My heart leaps with joy
Today my love will return
Life will start again.

The sky is cloudless
The hot sun beams down on us
You are beautiful.

Evening shadows fall
They cast a veil of sorrow
Please don't go away.

Tears flow from my eyes
Night-time has brought with it pain
Love has gone again.

Chris Hill

The Girl Without A Face

Unable to see,
Unable to breath
In that world so cruel and unstable.
A pleasant gift on one hand;
Being unable to see the evil
That men do; yet sometimes
It's necessary to tread on
Bloodied sand.

Christian Ward

A Country Walk

Oh what joy to stroll in the sun
Watch birds fluttering
From tree to tree
And observe them nesting
Till their task is done
Appearing contented
Happy and free
And to stroll near a stream
Where the fish
Swim to and fro
Then take a path
Through the wood
Where all the wild flowers grow
And eventually
Reaching a country lane
With no hint of cloud
Nor thundery rain
Oh what a joy it's been
To stroll in the sun
Amongst the wonders
Of nature
Where peace begun.

Edwin Jepson

Solitaire

Cards are drifting soft and slow
From her wrinkled parchment hand
Playing (mumbling selfward, low)
Solitaire.

Hustle! Bustle! All around her
Heedless, although they surround her
Sitting there.

One throws condescending glance,
'Poor old mindless crone,' he sniffs.
Leaves her, as he looks askance
In her chair.

Yet her memories replay on
Crowded card games of the past
Merry partners, now long gone
God knows where.

Tears blocked out of sunken eyes
Leaden hands place jack on queen
Staunching down her own soul cries . . .
No one cares.

This has become everything
Rest home's corner, silent, grey
Red ten, black jack, red queen, king . . .
Solitaire.

Mary Spence

Charlie - My Grandson!

Splash of light beyond the haze
Quells an intransient void.
How is it I gain so much from you,
My beauteous and wondrous boy?

Oh, how much you teach me
About unconditional love.
And if I eventually return to that state of innocence;
I have so much I owe to you,
My beauteous and wondrous boy.

David Lees

The Fox And Curs!

A group of foxes out one day
Thought they'd hunt some men
They'd found no fun in chickens
Locked inside a pen!
Chasing men was such a hoot!
But pursuers soon were caught
I fail to see the problem here
They were only making sport.

Marji Tomlinson

A Heap Of Stones

There it is in forlorned beauty,
Lone, drab and drear 'neath nettles' mask.
Where wild berries, black and fruity -
Wind, as painted ladies bask.
There, hidden and forgotten lies,
Beside a brook meand'ring by,
A remnant stony paradise -
Left unbelove'd, there to die.

Was it not a farmstead cluster,
And a garden full of flowers,
Where now sparrows chat, and muster -
In the elder tree for hours.
And was it not where butter churned -
The goodly pail of milk, each morn.
Where horses in bright harness, turned -
And reaped another row of corn.

Ah, was it so for many years -
Down by the stream, as I intone.
Where now the fox cub shyly peers,
Through ivy wreathe'd 'round a stone.
No longer in these fields there be -
The laughter of a child's delight.
Daisy chains are a memory,
Where harness clinks only at night.

Derek Haskett-Jones

At The Rainbow's End

The colours are slowly coming together
After all those frightening storms
Which blasted and frightened
Child, and adult, and all.

Let us not disturb this process
Which could take us to the highest plateau
On Earth - the mount of peace, which if taken,
Makes us our brother's keeper, and he ours.

Think hard on it Brother, even if it hurts
To descend to recrimination of one's self
No more difficult than a scrub-down of the soul.

Once cleansed, our inner selves will find no objection
To any colour that was inspired to form a rainbow,
Signalling the end of storms forever and with
Our maker create the happiest family on the planet
But we must let the cynic speak, 'It can't be done,'
And then notices a beautiful sunrise,
'But we must all give it a go!'

G R Doody

Secret Playmate

I've got a secret playmate
No one sees but me
He sits beside me at the table
When I sit down to tea

I call my playmate Robert
And he is only eight
I wish he'd eat my carrots up
'Cause they're something I really hate

He's with me in the garden
And we play hide-and-seek
He really is my best friend
Although he doesn't speak

I know my mum can't see him
But I know he's always there
Even when I'm sitting down
He's beside me on the chair

I love my secret playmate
And I'm never left alone
And as he always plays with me
I'm never on my own.

Anne Logan

Compulsion

Mathematical equations my life has known
With all possibilities with an overtone,
What number am I in a quantum test?
Let's queue for a variable at best
And write possibilities
To infinity and above
Life's not a number
It's what you make of it and love

Scientists scream with answers we all know
But come out with jargon
A tongue with no flow
They say we are all destined to become something
But who controls that the government and their
Function with no communication with lyrical
Consumption empty promises provide corruption.

So listen to this lyrical malfunction decide your fate
Your compunction to what is know by your understanding
Your life how you live and
Enjoy, it's now the beginning.

Paul D Blair

Still

Still stood in the rain
Still disturbed by the pain
Still envision your face
Still lost in this space
Still holding on
Still can't believe you're gone
Still in my dreams
Still my heart screams
Still on your side
Still nowhere to hide
Still lost and lonely
Still haven't phoned me
Still wait for your call
Still shocked by it all
Still no way of mending
Still no happy ending
Still tears running dry
Still wondering why
Still haven't been taught
Still glad I fought
Still won't pretend
Still can't let it end
Still no regrets
Still refuse to forget
Still do it again
Still worth all the pain
Still.

Lucy Sheldon

Dog Burning

I see dog burning,
in the corner of your sleep,
curled up in your eye,
untouched by searing flames.

The sky is commanding stone.
It triggers the sun out of devotion.
It wears a great coat to the funeral.

With me tractors, old stories,
woken up by farmers, soldiers.

The bottom of your lip is not healing.
Behind us, past the orchard, cotton fields,
the border, in separate air, unguarded.

Imprisoned in your smile,
we stand in a blue wilderness,
a burnt aftermath, a savage imagination.

Here is a desert, a sand kingdom, water provides.
We sip parched images, wet dry lips in paper wells.

Austin McCarron

Maybe

Songbuilt
By the toneplay of epiphany.

Merely a dictionary:
A rhyme-holed space in language.

Friday evening bath,
Water startles the pips to a conclusion.

Silence pre-empts an afterword;
My belated presence here
Makes singing slightly more
Difficult than listening.

A L Firth

Old School

You've kept it standing in line for twenty years,
still uniformed in utility council brick.
Old school pausing, until nostalgia thaws
in raw light during this late spring.
A stalled glance through the window
shows giddy paintings in primary colours,
sticky buds, closed fists in glue on
the nature table; all furniture half-size.
Yet all you recall is the scent of polish,
like incense in lit corridors going on endlessly.
It's as if these sparce details are dormant
like a chrysalis, folding memories around
empty days that remain vestigial.

Chris Todd

The Rain Feels Damp In My Hair

The rain feels damp in my hair
And all around
A thousand flies converge
To drink the sweat they smell.

The trees bend forward their boughs
Intent on blocking the sun
That dares to peep between the cracks
In those depressing clouds.

So it ever was beside the lake
For was it ever fine?
Not in my memory
There was never a time.

I see the waters deep
Where once a hundred voices sang
Cwm Rhondda beneath the silent spire,
Every woman and her man.

And at the edge I hear
The voices yet again from days gone by
When they and I were young
The mirror in the water cannot lie.

Wafting on the breeze
Across the water
Sounds so rich and splendid
The choir of Kenfig.

I see them against the background sky
Dancing in the shimmering water
Yet clear to my old eye
Each woman, man and daughter.

As if in silent shame
The image sinks away,
Then all is eerie quiet
Except the persistent rain.

C O Burnell

Hello Life

Hello life once again
I want to embrace you,
My touch may be poison
My soul unclean,
I need my arms around you
But not to contaminate,
Let me see you
In all your glory,
I am not worthy
Of the compassion
That Mother Nature shows,
The miracles of life
The air that we breathe,
Of the sun that rises
Or the moon at night,
My strength is not strong enough
For you're mighty capacity,
I am weak of spirit
I am weak of mind,
Too sad for this world
Too bad for this life.

Kathryn Evans

The Plastic Card

Some man, it must have been a man
Brought forth a new invention
It was of course the plastic card
To make life easier was his intention
We have cards to do the shopping
Cards to borrow books and tapes
Cards to do the banking
In the hopes that at least it makes
Life a little easier for each and everyone
But in fact it is not so
Because in the end we have become
A nation of plastic card carriers
And we cannot seem to choose
Just told you must look after it
Keep it safe and do not lose
The stress and trauma that they bring
To your head is very hard
When one day you finally know
You cannot find your plastic card
Plastic cards bring happiness
They also bring great sorrow
So I think I'll take the scissors to
My plastic cards tomorrow.

D Fryer

On The Death Of A Wife

She has fled . . .
The flowers have faded,
The leaves have fallen,
The birds have flown;
The earth is frozen;
Nothing is left . . .
Only sorrow.

Muriel Willa

Time

Time is an elusive thing
That no one can hold on to.
It marches on its own sweet way
People drowning in its wake.

Why do we delude ourselves
That we have so much of it?
Putting off from day to day
All the things you mean to do
From a mixture of laziness and fear.

'Seize the moment,' someone said or I read,
'Yeah yeah tomorrow,' I said.
Too many tomorrows became
Too many yesterdays I did not seize
Now all that's left are empty memories.

Linda Dobinson

The Country Road

As I slowly walk along
This winding country road
I remember the happy times
When I walked hand in hand
Along this country road
With an angel of beauty
Called Yvonne Burnnip.

But no longer do I know
Where that angel now lives
For one day she said goodbye to me
Then walked out of my life forever
And that's why I now walk
Along this country road
So sad and all alone
And a life filled full
Of pain and sorrow
For no more happy tomorrows
Will I ever have
Without that angel of beauty
Walking by my side.

Donald John Tye

The Cockerel

The cockerel in his splendid plumage,
golden browns, iridescent greens and blues
bright red crown and crop,
yellow scaly legs and feet with polished
ivory curved nails.
One foot poised mid-air.
Head turned and cocked to side.
Bright amber eye alert.

Chickens pecking and scratching between
rows of black and red currants, peas and beans,
enjoy the freedom denied to their owner.
One would be chosen this week for Sunday dinner.
Ushered into back yard.
Head held tight and put on block.
Axe brought down on scrawny neck.
Body twitching, bloody head jumping,
spinning like a multicoloured top.

Anne Jenkins

What Is Happening To Me?

How blue the sky is, and
how did I come to be here
lying on my back in the
filth and mud. I look up
once more, what was that
whizzing by? What is happening
to me? Was it a bird or a bullet
for another guy? I cannot tell for
I don't see so well.

My bones feel cold, and yet
there is no pain, it will be
all right when I stand up again,
Why don't these legs of mine
work, it must be the boots.
Strange, the sky is not blue
anymore. What is happening to me?
Why did that man shriek and
call for Mother? Oh Lord, tell him to
stop, it sounds like me.

I turn my head, and I see
someone's legs. Whose can they be?
I hope they're not mine.
Now darkness descends like a friend
and sleep is peace at last for me.

J L Holden

The Swallows

(Written while serving with the South African infantry in North Africa 1939-45)

Back, to the swarm-lands of the south
the swallows fly;
back to the south land where sigh on sigh
come on a sea wind.
O, if the swallows be flying,
why cannot I?

But I am doomed to hear the old sea breaking
my heart to pieces. Each year the swallows higher
and higher soar,
and futher seems the flight they are making
to the drawn face which I shall see no more
until I die.

Charles Ernest Cumings

Going West

The sun is heating now beating down
And I'm far away from my hometown
Mostly empty barren land that surrounds
All around my travels the heat has been dry
I see in the north the mountains are high
And a deep valley and hills on both sides
It's the same when the sun sets to the sunrise
The path is long, almost seems forever
All the way I feel the hard-hitting weather
The days are seen longer and the nights are shorter
Going west for the best to the western border
It's like a dry desert I need food and water.

Away to a new country, I feel hot and hungry
I've been secretly silenced by this long journey
I've been walking for thousands of miles
I've been walking for thousands of years
My destiny, fate has it, is the British Isles
I've lived most of my years in great fear
I've been through *hell* just to get here
Left my mother country and my mother tongue
This wasn't the dream I had when I was young
It's a long rainy slave song that's now been sung
Going west for the best to the western border
It's like a dry desert I need food and water

Across the seven seas I survived the ships
I survived the iron chains and leather whips
I survived the government and its foreign policy tricks
I went through harsh gale force winds
Stormy days and nights like a stowaway
From beggar, a pauper to would be kings
Looking to see the brightest sun in array
Who knows what life might bring
A new dawn breeds another new day
Now the nights are longer and the days are shorter
I've come west to see what's best across the western border
At my destination I finally, get some food and water.

Dharminder Gill

A Night Of Evil

The darkness gathers them to its soul
Whilst we citizens, shiver with fright
They crawl and emerge, from the deepest hole
All the doors are locked, on this terrible night.

Frightened glances, as we hear the wind howl
They will be performing the Devil's work
From the kitchen, comes my faithful dog's growl
Outside numerous premises, they will lurk.

Faces which, in mirrors, cannot be seen
Monstrous footprints, left in the ground
One-eyed monsters, with oily skins of green
And evil creatures that fly, with no sound.

Not in any house, will a light shine
Some people will hide under a bed
Tomorrow morning, everything will be fine
When all these monstrosities have fled.

They'll get no answer, if they ring our bell
We're too busy, holding each other tight
Go back to the cavities, where you usually dwell
And stop putting us through this terrible plight.

We know, on this night, we will get no sleep
At least not before the early hours of dawn
Around the streets these foul things will creep
Some of them possess a nasty spiked horn.

And I have no weapons to defend
My family and myself, from this hell
Upon my friend up above, I must depend
That we struggle through this horrific spell.

This Hallowe'en night, every year, which I cannot defeat
For weeks after, I have this dreaded fear, remembering, *'Trick or treat'*.

B W Ballard

Weight Watchers

She's getting fatter
Fatter and fatter
Cos she's eating chips
And fish in batter
While she's eating up
Her daily load
Maybe some time soon
Maybe she'll explode
Down the toilet
After stuffing her cake hole
Down the toilet
After stuffing a meat roll
There's lots to eat
There's lots of meat
So go bake us up
Some massive treat

J J Georgion

Untitled

When a beautiful scent
Flows in the air
When another sun shines
With brighter glare
When I'm in a heaven
No one could ever see
I know you're coming to me

Haitham Hafez

Velvet Memories

Cast your mind back
To childhood and the beach
Where tales were like waves
And mystery held us enthralled

Your were my mermaid
Washed upon sands
Beyond the hands
Of the waves and tides

Cast about you
Were your clothes of weed
And tangled seashell
There upon the tide-swept sands

I turned about to find
That we were not alone
For other shadowy figures
Had gathered on the shingle bank

They gazed in ignorance
And a lack of understanding
Of the magic we had created
Beyond the edges of this world

I wrapped my cloak about you
And led you from the scene,
Past their faces, past their eyes,
For these were our velvet memories.

Richard Gould

Smith

Large brown eyes rolling in frustration
She ponders the question sincerely
Her touch so tender and sensuous
Mind sharp, aware of circumstance

Want, had become desire
Desire, surpassed by pure passion
Common sense prevailing quickly
Indecision terminated with gentle conversation

The time together had been magical
Infatuation no longer a dream
Reality making moments surreal
A bond built for the future

She left, as a different person
Secure in her self-belief and confidence
Knowing her time would arrive shortly
Total bonding completed with just one kiss

Alan Zoltie

Dear Long-Lost Lover

Turn out the daylight
Cover it in clouds
Wipe off my smiles
For I cry out loud.

Strip the trees of their leaves
Turn them autumn brown
Why is it when you start to feel up
You always come back down?

Steal the waves from the sea and make it still
Look inside an empty box
And see how I feel.

Take the grapes from the wine
Turn it to water
Take away my support
And see me falter.

Tear the pages from the book
My dear long-lost lover
For all that remains now
Is an old empty cover.

Dawn Colley

A Fool Finally

Heartaches aside, today
is April Fool's Day.
When nobody should be hurt
by a practical joke.
Falling in love is like
becoming a fool finally.
A sad state of affairs.

Kirk Antony Watson

Oxford Movement

Two clergymen, Newman and Pusey,
accosted one day by a floozy,
warned her, 'Madame, we're vicars,'
but she whipped off her knickers,
saying, 'That's all right luvs, I'm not choosy.'

Norman Bissett

Shelter Island - 1976, 1981, 1990

Observed I

A star big as earth
blocked by a firefly,
a lighthouse.

Observed II

Seen from the cliff;
a seagull and its reflection.
A kite and its shadow.

Observed III

Usually
seaweed writes in lines
passive and orderly:
signature of tides.

This storm has
scribbled them,
tossed hieroglyphs and runes,
Arabic characters,
ideographs. Codes.

Ellen Peckham

A Few Specks

As I sit and watch the clouds rolling by,
Great white shape shifters traversing the sky,
I see a jet plane,
A mere speck!

I think of myself, as I sit here looking around,
And watch the ant on its busy way, ant nest bound,
To me, the ant,
A mere speck!

When I think of the Earth and then I see
Pictures of our universe, or a single galaxy,
Then our Earth seems also,
A mere speck!

A teardrop falling on my knee,
If that same teardrop fell into the sea,
Lost from here to infinity,
A mere speck!

What a great word, a great sound, *infinity,*
Beyond comprehension, beyond imagination maybe,
But in a whole dictionary,
A mere speck!

Underneath a microscope, laid upon a slide,
What is this many-legged beast with a hairy hide,
A corn fly, to the naked eye,
A mere speck!

I could go on and on, and end up boring everyone,
A few pages scattered in a forest, timber weighing nearly a ton,
A few pages, a mere speck!

Christine Turner

Punk

tall, short, fat, skinny, black or white
no matter who you are you still
can be a punk, punks are cool
you can be Christian or not
you still can be one, listen to
punk music or that's punkish
to you, punks wear punkish
clothes, shoes etc, if you've
got the punk in you
give it
        to the punks out there.

Zach Budnick

Personal Hell

My soul lies shaking in the shadows of my personal hell.
Is there any light in here and if so, my soul I'd sell.
Welcome to my bad dream, where nothing is quite as it may seem.
Come into my world, where all that's good is taken and hurled.
There's no happy thoughts here.
Everything is evil and pain is always near.
Darkened hearts are all around.
Screaming echoes with every sound.
Welcome to my existence, where pain is lurking and can come
in an instance.
I hope your life has love that won't turn back.
My love is far behind me and my heart's turning black.

Chris Flett

River Of Light

Rain across the windowpane
Tumbling to the window sill
A trail left for others to follow
They catch up, merge into one
Then drop making a deluge
Light cascading sparkling as they fall
Rivers of light.

Carole A Cleverdon

What's Up?

Toast it tomorrow
With a touch of garlic
To help digestion
So you can watch news
And TV again and again
Yawn into the silence
Of the breaking wars
Raging inside your mind
As they fill it up
As if your mind was a car
It never leaves you alone
And you forget yourself

And then you wonder
What's up with the world?

Petra Whiteley

Blanket Of Protection

Forever moving slowly
Like snails in the sky
They glide softly together
Side by side
One above the other
A blanket, division
A form of protection
Keeping us from the unknown
A carpet for others to tread
We can only look up and admire
An army of whiteness
Relaxed and collective
There to see but not to touch
Taking on different forms
A horse! A chariot!
An eagle! A clarinet!
Shifting from shape to shape
Before slowly disappearing
Carrying with it the light from above
Holding down the dark from below.

Chris Campbell

Wayward Ways With Words

Politicians and journalists frequently reach
For some of their favourite figures of speech.
So much have some sayings been bandied about,
That they are irritating for being so worn out.
Adopting one of them, I say, 'Let's move on.'
I'd be glad if that, and others like it, were gone.
My wish applies also to 'drawing a line'
(As to which, look in Anchor Books' 'Reach Beyond Time',
A title which prompts recollection of how
'At this moment in time' has replaced simply 'now').
In the same sort of context, I've noticed a trend
To appeal for a 'closure'; what's wrong with 'an end'?
The word 'frightening' seems to be no longer said;
People prefer to say 'scary' instead;
And are you, dear reader, becoming aware
That the public are often described as 'out there'?

Some changes in rhythm are the only ways
By which I can mention a few more clichés.

'The negotiating table' is in regular demand
For the parties, to disputes within, and far beyond, this land;
If I were in removals, I could make a 'tidy' pound
From a money-making contract for transporting it around.
'A window of opportunity' is uttered to enhance
The comments of some speakers; why not call it just 'a chance'?
The Government are said to have 'a package' on 'a raft'
Of measures; saying 'parcel' or 'canoe' would be as daft.

I know that language is a 'living' thing, but that does not excuse
The superfluous and idiotic terms which people use.

Anthony Hofler

Doting Parents

My parents loved me far too much,
Their fingers in my pie,
Their need was great and taking such,
I found I'd been sucked dry.

My life accommodates their needs,
Their need is not for me,
To blossom, flourish, fly away,
They'll never set me free.

My children came to be for them,
Their destiny fulfilled,
And I am spent from one to ten,
No longer needed, killed.

Kisses, cuddles lavished, spoilt,
Little madams made,
And I am left to clear the mess,
My value simply fades.

Can you see me? Am I here?
Or do I simply give,
For everyone to take from me,
A happier life to live?

Sarah Dixon

A Longing

Oh to be in Ireland now that
    April's there
For whoever wakes in an
    Irish morn
Is enchantingly aware,
Of magic sight when the
    mists unfold,
As the dewdrops catch the
    first sunbeam
Suspended on a nocturnal
    spider's silvery skein
Changing them slowly
    into gold.
The sweet song thrush
    greets the new day
Perched on lofty
    holly bough
And the soft wind ruffles
    the sally leaves
In lovely Ireland now.
And when April, loath to
    leave - departs
To make room for apple
    blossom May,
Swallows swoop and
    swerve in a clear blue sky
At their courtship interplay.
The mountains shed their
    wintry overcoats
And don their mantle
    of green,
While sweet golden
    buttercups, and wild
    daisies' throats
To the sun their
    petals preen.
As I watch the wild geese
    homeward bound

And pause to wipe my brow
How I wish that I could fly
    like them
To lovely Ireland now.

Mike Tatten

Big Brother Seraphin

The child full of sorrow,
Weeps a tear from each eye,
Whilst Big Brother Seraphin,
Looks down from on high.
He understands the sadness,
He understands the pain,
He lets the child know he's there
And calls aloud his name.

The child sees a star above
And looks into the sky,
Whilst Big Brother Seraphin
Looks down from on high.
He takes away the sadness
And buries all the pain
Then attends another cry
To start his work again.

Tony Pratt

Strange Experiences On Visiting The Himalayan Region

I had an opportunity wholesome
To visit the mysterious grandeur
Of the Himalayan range of mountains,
Along with some of my friends and relatives;
It's a strange experience
To feel how the long-drawn
Snow-clad peaks stand high, majestic
In the tremendous sunshine beauties;
To me it was another world
Of the eagle - the world of fierce abstraction!
An eagle kept rounding and rounding
For several times in the sunshine overwhelming,
And disappeared like the golden light
Of hopefulness and blessedness into Heaven!
It was all clear above, and I was as if,
In a platform hung in the world of light!
Just below were the confused
Tiled roofs of villages,
And beyond them the pale blue water
Of a swift stream sparkling far down below.
I felt myself in the skies now
In the world of brightness!
In contrast, inside the church
Was very dark, impregnated with centuries
Of incense, yet my senses
Sprang awake in the hot-spiced darkness
In deep adoration for Holy Graces divine.
But my soul got liberated in the marvellous
Clarity of sunshine, in the upper half
Of the mountain brilliantly white
With snow dazzling in the sun brightening,
While the lower half, dark and grim,
For the green forest grand enclosing.
The blue Heaven in that light
Seemed to distil me into itself!

Kalyan Ray

Purifier

She's a wall,
a tower of strength.
The more something means,
the more I shout and bellow.
The more I speak of my
broken dreams again,
the more she stands, strong
and complete, absorbing,
containing more than ever.

She's lost her temper before
of course, but there's always
a point, and I usually learn
something I should have learned
before, there's a story in all.

She gets her composure back
and pulls me together.
As we talk quietly together, in
the strange calm after the storm
more information, and with a
greater detail, comes pouring
forth. Old divisions are healed
and possibly some new created.
But all seems well at the time of
asking, so we move on replete
of old complaints.
If we are lucky, it will complete
the balance between us again
and maintain the purity between us.

David Finlay

A Poem For Ash Wednesday

It is Ash Wednesday as I kneel, pray:
Behold, I see a new Jerusalem,
The worlds of light upon walls, high,
Of love, of worlds, yet unseen, of Heaven;
I read the eternal scripture written,
A biblical, spiritual delight:
Our Lady, language stands above
The laws of evil, a wonderful,
Holy waterfall, above the tragic
Madness upon the Earth. O look, a new
Jerusalem, behold I see that bright
New name written there, in love, holy
Words of wonder cascade in prayer:
Behold, I read a new Jerusalem,
As I kneel and pray on Ash Wednesday.

Edmund Saint George Mooney

Personal Hell

Varying shades
of darkness
echo the misery
of my soul.
Colourful crescendos
that were
are now a paler hue.
All remembrances
of what was
dimming of reality
yet flourishing
the thought,
the misery,
the anguish,
my mind -
a raging pool
of thoughts
of days gone past
so full of hope,
but now so bleak.
The future speaks,
I see no reprieve,
condemned!
For sure . . .
it's hell!

Jillian A Nagra

Firecracker

With a selfless, doubtless heart
She was his firecracker -
All ponytails and grassy knees.

And when five chubby digits
Reached out for powerful hands -
He was master of this land.

Monsters prowled through trees
Of forests knee-high to him -
As she explored her jungle world.

A break for dinner met with tears
As bread and cheese were shared
Between this intrepid duo.

Years passed and competition came
In the form of inappropriate men -
With names like Scott and Joe.

And Firecracker wiped her tears
Burying her swollen red eyes
In familiar smelling T-shirts.

But she learnt from loving play
And became the woman he grew -
With eyes as good as his.

So now he happily waits at home
For the familiar voice to say -
That Firecracker's home.

Jude Lynskey

The Old Town Wears Strong Perfume

The old town wears strong perfume,
rubbish dump, The Ship and fried fish;
The Sun slipped and wrapped round hot brown chips.

Tea steam,
the smoke,
blown from the deer park
on golden wind.

Petrol, cut grass,
the smell of smoke.

Cut grass,
the smoke,
the smell of cedar wood.

Old sweat,
tea steam,
blue smell of cigar smoke.

The Sun slipped and wrapped round battered fish,
bubble gum, the pub and fried chips;
this old town wears strong perfume.

Jonathan Chant

Smell

The stench of fear was in the air
No one helped
No one wanted
Everybody saw
What was happening
Silent participants
To crimes
On a mega scale
Damaged adults
Walking
Preying
On damaged adults
Everyone trying to be boss
Everyone trying to outdo each other
Playground rules applied

Kauser Parveen

Creativity

The best poems
are usually chiselled
and elegant,
like lilies growing straight
towards the sky,
and sky-coloured
- or they are cupped
like a rose,
with such a heavy scent
that you swoon.

But some are often
like seedlings, eager
to show themselves,
but trampled
under hobnailed boots;

or else they grow
like potatoes or parsnips
uncertain of shape
quite tasty at times

but growing
under
ground.

David C Taylor

Hamlet And Caesar

Say yes, turn your back and leave
as it was always meant to happen,
as we both knew it would end,
I am lovely Prince Hamlet, and was so meant to be
or not to be.
And you,
you are Julius Caesar.
And we were too different to be in love
(both tragic heroes and all
realising our faults at the last minute,
or maybe that was just me?)
So, now you'll leave me on a balcony overlooking an
                                        Italian courtyard,
don't bother to say goodbye (parting is such . . . sorrow).
Knowing you (which I don't), you won't say anything.
You were already packing,
planning your escape,
before you knew you'd leave.
You were too beautiful for this world, so you left it.
And now, Laertes begins my duel, and Brutus is behind you,
killed by fealty and arrogance respectively, but:
If ever didst thee in thy heart hold me dear,
Thou wilt not leave it at this.
Thou wilt not leave.

Emerson Richards

Naked Envy

I cannot touch the juicy fruit
However tempting it may be
It is sold to one more suitable
And there are others to conceive
Typical of spiteful dreams
The nicest fruit is out of reach and beyond my means
Hers not mine
The lucky witch
I hope she looks a fright
Not a shrouded beauty
It gives me comfort on the lonely nights

Bryony Freeman

Wave

Life like a ripple in a pond,
Or the great waves of the sea.

Any one of which could pass you by
Or crush you down into a grain of salt,
Joining you and the great sea of tears of those who feel the waves.

The ocean froths at the mouth and swirls!
Like a blue-eyed girl with a cold, dead heart.
Cold and bitter,
Like a rusty blade pushed into your side,
Washed with a wave of sea, salt and sand.

Don't cry! Don't add to this sea.
Blue is so full of sorrow and fear!

Don't you wish the sea was red?

Steven Thurlow

A Life Through A Pen

Words so meaningless, they roll right off the page
Intensity always muffled by another age
Trying so hard, to overcome the fall
Topping yourself up with endless scribble and scrawl
So I watch your ink loop and coil
As you cook up more words and set them to boil
But by pen the world will never hear your scream
Never know enough to wake you from this dream
Turning the pages of my memory, I see it in your eyes
You too drifted silently, temporarily entranced by lullabies
Then have the same scar etched in your brain
What it's like to be labelled 'beyond insane'?

Pick up this nib, watch my soul streaming out
Sick images slide further, impossible not to think about
Contemplate disowning yourself, just so you can pretend
Wounds - gaps, filling me up, begging you to mend
Red ink contrasting with a numbing smile
Thinking over the words that blinded me all the while
Your eyes seem bright but stretched to a smear
I hold up the page - to display your fear
Shut off your mind
Escape to the rind
Where all is shaded, yet in every way true
With a pen in my hand I wash myself of you

My name is called, I enter the room
Hoping this will be over soon
Cover my face, so you can't see
That those words belong to me
Not my mind . . . not my page
Those words still muffled by another age
Don't talk to me, you don't know
No empathy please, just let me go

Emily Wiltshire

Friends

Friends are special, they are there
For each other, through thick and thin.
Friends are friends to the end.
If you had everything you wished for
But had no friends, then you would have nothing.
I would rather have nothing and have friends.
No matter what distance there is between friends,
No matter what obstacles get in the way,
Friends are friends forever.

C J Walls

Sad In A Funny Way

I am funny in a sad sort of way,
Like rally, tragically, on the border of, gay.
I look like a female she said, and
She put me in a swish silver skirt.
The hat didn't match, but like I said:
I am sad in a funny sort of way.
She giggled like I was hysterical,
I made that nonsense sound, and she
Threatened; my own section in the hospital.
She stopped laughing and scoffed, saying,
'I am funny in a sad sort of way.'
Had she read my mind I wondered?
Guessing, to share this thought would,
Be as bright as the bottom of a closed coal mine.
Even thicko old me can see that
I am funny in a sad sort of way.

James Midgley

The Path

(In memory of Muriel Pike 18/5/05)

Glorious is the path we tread
Each step to be enjoyed
Rich pleasures gained as the path meanders,
Treasured memories they remain

Weep not dear friends,
Life still goes on
In glory each new day
Sing, be happy, and recall the path
Of joyous, and lasting memories.

Elizabeth Hayden-Jones

Concentration

Thought's geometry
is engineered into
a field of force from the tip
of the pen to your eye and shoulder,
sustained by the taut cables
of your task.
              One more heave and strain
will show the strength of the frame,
part the dull unworked earth
from your winged understanding.

I wait, a spectator to discovery
whose moment of revelation
is to see the whole world refocus
in your face when you look up
as though recalling a vision.

Mark James Leech

Prolific

Dear Mr/Mrs Muse,
Please keep them coming,
All these poems.
How about some stories, too?
Even a novel? Or is that too much
To ask?
I answer myself, *it is too much.*
Yet, being a writer remains
A blessing - never quite
A curse.
Yeah, right.

Michelle Louisa Corp

Lost Youth

Once so fresh, so radiant
a blessing swiftly snatched away.
Beauty replaced unwontedly,
I no longer know nor want you.

If I could run, I would
a blessing swiftly snatched away.
Health so sadly deteriorated
trapped in an enemy tomb.

The youth I once owned
a blessing swiftly snatched away.
Cruelly paraded before me
refusing to acknowledge my existence.

A momentary relief! Ah, memories!
My blessings swiftly return my way,
only to be quickly sent packing
by the sneer and mocks of my reflection.

Susan Macdougal

Mama

(To Caroline Adjapomaa Kwayisi . . . for the values we hold dear)

May I cry for you Mama, Mama may I cry?

Nine months I crouched in you waiting to see what the future holds.
You played the waiting game hoping and wishing that I may be.

Then came the first sound the day you will come to ever cherish
Young as I was I could only cause you pain, the truancy
Here I stand willing and hoping to repair and repay.
If I fail, Mama, I will cry, I will cry because I want to.

Now old I see traces but how long will I wait to go places? I wish,
I could control the contorted dear Mama.

I look in hindsight with frustration and foresight with desperation.
How I wish I could do more. I will not rest until I do best.
To end it all I have to begin.
Forgive me Mama if I cry because I want to.

Samuel Ofosuhene

Good Evening Officer

I might have had a couple
More than one or two,
Six or seven come to mind
It was quite a few.
That was just the pints of ale,
Foaming, crisp and clear.
After that came whisky,
I didn't want more beer.
Then I had some wine as well,
Grape and grain don't mix.
Don't remember eating,
That's why I'm in this fix.

But I don't care what you think.
I don't give a damn,
Because I know I'm not as thrunk
As drinkle peep I am.

Chris Smith

So Scared

I am so scared.
I don't know how
To ease this frightening fear.
I just want someone to be there.
Someone to tell me
It's all right.
I know that it's not.
But that's what I need
To keep me from
Feeling so scared.

I need someone
To hold me, and cry
With me.
Tell me that things
Will get better.
That I will not always
Be this scared.
That there is
'Light at the end of the tunnel'.
I hate feeling so scared.
But I hate feeling alone
So much more.

Is asking for someone
To tell me not to be so scared
Too much to ask for?
Am I being selfish?
I hope not,
Because I am scared enough
As it is.

Carol Arnold

Untitled

Bright light stripping wood
Glancing off luminous metal
Like rays straight from the sun itself.
So goes the expounding, expanding heat
Filtering into the heavy head
Lost in its pure thoughts of loneliness.
She lies in her own blood
Without the other half.
He wanders through it all
Ignorant as to why
That missing rib is still missing.
A foot without the other is not feet
So goes eyes, ears, hands, and legs.
In pairs the world is created
The sweet sanctimony of twos
One makes up for what the other lacks.
The duality of nature
In its birth and its death
Pounding through the soul of the universe.

Reena Devi Shanmuga Retnam

Poem

I want you to know all the secrets inside me,
I found them when sailing and looking for shore.
Instead what I saw was the sky meet the sea,
And the clouds disappear in the sun.

Where wave upon wave of ocean and sky
Are knitted together with an invisible seam,
For no more than a second, a lifetime in brief,
I danced on the water and swam in the sky.

I knew I could tell you by the way that I saw you,
Walking with someone looking for more.
You knew by the way I sat like a sculpture,
Soul of an artist and drinking for fun.

Prancing round the castle was a girl who laughed when lying,
Waving sheets around her - coloured crimson and gold.
She believed in magic, so I told her I do too,
Nothing was to change; but you forgot how to look at me.

Contingent on my name are the letters of yours.
I'll always believe you, as you will that.
Though settled in ink with a smile from the state,
Will be your replacement for a poet's mistake.

Michael Pedersen

Mischievous

There's a band of teasing imps
Yelling crazy just out there.
Went to peep them through the trees
One of them held on his back
The wreck of a yellow door
A girl was, I can swear to you
- Dressed with the dress of a whore -
Kicking his ass to get fun.
On the door were three green frogs
I had not seen at first sight
Loudly singing bawdy songs.
Another one with Sam's flag
As a cloak on his shoulders
Was playing a saxophone
Hitting flowers with wrong notes.
I won't tell you about how
Two of them were in the sun
Having the best things of life.
I would like, but imagine
In case it was read by Mum!
A seven-legged pollywog
Was jumping at naked girls
Who were smoking in the fog
So sweet-smelling cigarettes
It made me feel like trying
That's why I now keep singing,
'There's a band of teasing imps
Yelling crazy just out there.'

Marie Rennard

A Thousand Places . . .

A helpless little soul,
Struggling to keep her head held high,
She has a thousand places to see, before she dies . . .

A world full of nothingness,
A constant clinging to hopes and desires,
She has a thousand places to see, before she dies . . .

Sweet love trickles slowly,
But when it's almost there, it somehow runs dry
She has a thousand places to see, before she dies . . .

Her hands were clasped tightly,
But her fingers couldn't fight
She has a thousand places to see, before she dies . . .

And then she gropes in the darkness,
Forgetting what is light,
She has a thousand places to see, before she dies . . .

Silent screams become softer,
A voice buried inside,
She has a thousand places to see, before she dies . . .

No words are ever spoken
She can never explain her heart's cry,
She has a thousand places to see, before she dies . . .

But she has a precious, precious treasure,
Can love like magic
And dream like a child

But a cry each day, that it never runs dry

I'm sure she will go a thousand places, before she dies . . .

Kinjal Desai

And So Awakens

Mid afternoon flows breeze
Under the apple tree below
Busy now waiter calls, 'Hello'
On seeing entrenched views
Awaken the early bliss from me
Like so many times before
And who stood by you then?
Only thy human self or so
One more refugee from war
Until the taunts destroyed him
The prison of universe springs

Malachy Trainor

My Sweet Soulmate

I've watched your footsteps,
sleekly meander that cools my heart
over several seasons.

I've savoured your beauty,
elegance clothed in sensibility
these long harmless years.

I've sat alone
in the pit of thoughts
probed the elation
that encompasses us
each time we're warmly entwined.

I've held you tenderly,
kissed you passionately,
passion that clings like
tendrils lining a tree.

I've mumbled affectionate words
into your lovely ears,
your sensitive ears that
absolve my poetic drumbeats.

The aroma of your love,
a whiff that makes heady,
it dazes like strong wine
as my soul sways with tenderness.

My sweet soulmate . . .

Emeka Chike Nwogu

The Lovestruck Fluff-Fall

(A very serious poem)

Asked the lovestruck fluff-fall of the itchysnitch,
'By what name dost that chalmangrous archepalien go?
Thinks I, a name of semphatical sensuousity
A beau-beau name, poetical and harmeryl.'
Replied the itchysnitch,
'Beryl.'

Richard Mathews

The Decision

Though well-equipped to my eyebrow,
to him a naïve.
His foundation little match for mine.
Steadfast in his staunch principle
he trained me and mocked my simplicity.
His directions addictive,
I heavily relied upon his manner
and lost myself along the way.

I let him detract me
pinned in a dreary storm,
welded by shackles of stony beliefs.
Was drowned in a flood of my own doing,
only my eyes the bystander
to dull the darkness within.
I painstakingly disentangled
and relearned to discover 'I'.

Frantic, I realised, such carnage
of strength and creativity.
The freedom to be oneself -
an absolute fulfilment.
A mocking mouth left wide open.
I note; when we decide change will follow.
My changing set afloat, change in others
without the need to change them.
God in all things; is waiting, encouraging.

Yasmeen Ahmed

Ashes

Leaving me alone; remorse
against your memories, cast adrift.
How I cried, wanting more,
reborn in desire your ashes.
You are ashes . . .

All I can remember, is that you lied
your sweet lies; eddying waves, rippled onto shore.
Promised life eternal; then died
like you; they are no more.
Leaving me alone with - your ashes . . .

My anger, thrown back into the seas, molten ink
unfathomable silence; a raging sea spray.
Floating seaweed began to pop and stink,
even as it cracked and split; like my heart today.
Remorse against - your ashes . . .

Silver stars pierce my selfish thoughts
a freezing pink fog that burns.
Bleaching grey; the red rose and orange lily ports
my mind, an unlit crystal sea that yearns.
Memories cast adrift among - your ashes . . .

Telling of my sorrow to Heaven above
the black heart, of a blue moon; on the rolling tide
Even as my emotions slip and slide
sending him kisses; my poor cold love.
How I cried for - your ashes . . .

Once again, I find myself among
gentle waves; mirrored in the early morning tide.
And the wet sand I'm standing on
knows, I can't join you: on this final ride.
Wanting more from - your ashes . . .

My hope driftwood, on the shoreline
until daybreak, the climbing sun high overhead.
Told tales in rock pools. A greater divine
of water and light and I knew, you were not dead.
Reborn in desire - your ashes . . .

Mary Jane Evans

Dear Forrester

I was very foolish was I
Yes me
I didn't see you then
Only, I see you now

The moon sits above me
As if lighting my realisation
For not just me to see
But for you

It's all you dear Forrester
My dreams are all you

Caem Humphries

Check Them They Wreck Them

with names sounding good
any crime can be committed
they just alter records

we all had to measure her
from that angle you can see two fingers

I'm rising doubts about Anna's sanity
and so have a non-stop array of voices

destroy her old age insurance
if she's not here what is the difference

it's my project it is my little programme
we've got carte blanche to kill and maim

beggar them criminalise them drugs anything
the country is turning a blind eye

we caused a lot of crime in Sheffield
we'd better apologise and talk to the Postmaster

anything is possible anything is permissible
we just have to say thank you

not even beads?
but your poetry will never see the light of day . . .

Renate Fekete

Drugs

Man's modern substances,
One for all circumstances,
Especially disco dances,
Make for an occasion,
Of chemical ecstasy,
Fuel the fusion of internal raving,
Till bugger up the consequences of crazy paving,
Hyped up, psyched up and depraving,
We snort the white powder,
And sing louder and louder,
Until we believe the country we're saving,
The pubs are packed, the nerves are wracked,
We are on the jazz, the razzamatazz,
After a whole weekend of narcotic slaving,
It's a white powder like Ariel, Daz,
Zodiac twisted faces like tongues,
Denim crutches groped, toke toked,
Down death dreaming in the afternoon,
Here's Lisa, she's a slut from a cartoon,
She's an easy lay if you can come down,
And stop whizzing the talk like a demented clown.

F Hilton

Memento

The fingertip stepping round the rim
of a light, a lamp of certain dimension
of a certain colour, chosen for a long ago
scene, as if it, less now,
is a bite, bitten from its rim, its side
through a move. How did the travel scene change
and pots rearrange themselves and yet
bites remain as reminders?

Better times perhaps in some ways. Well, not so much.
They serve a glimmer, set in state of habit, inner certitude.

And I? The solid lamp remains a memento
of a pain that wasn't once.

Diane Burrow

Cover Me In Roses

(Love song)

So cover me in roses girl and say your name aloud,
And do the magic of your sun dance,
It's a thrill to hear your heartbeat, beating next to mine,
That sounds like a poet's loving rhyme,
In all those years I wanted you with undying passion,
To love you eternally forever more,
With the scent and perfume that you wear,
Only God knows how I feel when I kiss your honey-coated lips,
In summertime all the bees and birds are in flight,
Now Heaven's got me singing this beautiful love song,
While I lay dreaming of your ghostly shadow,
And my heart is homebound waiting yours,
So baby come quickly this midnight hour,
And love me with your triumphant smile,
So cover me in roses girl and say your name aloud,
And do the magic of your sun dance,
It's a thrill to hear your heartbeat, beating next to mine,
That sounds like a poet's loving rhyme,
In all these years I wanted you with undying passion,
No one knows how I really feel, but you girl, only you girl,
Like a flying angel come down from Heaven, I love you girl,
More than any words can deliver, oh girl,
You're my only dying wish, you're my only dying wish,
To love you eternally forever more,
With the scent and perfume that you wear,
Only God knows how I feel when I kiss your honey-coated lips,
In summertime all the bees and birds are in flight,
Now Heaven's got me singing this beautiful love song,
While I lay dreaming of your ghostly shadow,
So cover me in roses girl and say your name aloud,
And do the magic of your sun dance,
It's a thrill to hear your heartbeat, beating next to mine.

James Stephen Cameron

Winter

As time passes by the piglets grow
Through spring, through summer, autumn and snow
When the first snowflakes appeared on the ground
Percival's eyes with wonder were round.

He cautiously put out a trotter to feel
And then he snuffled and oinked with zeal,
'It's vanished gain, where's it gone?' he said,
And fetched his brothers from their bed.

Then the snow came thick and fast
Said Farmer George, 'It's going to last
We'll need to get the barn cleared out
The animals in, without a doubt.'

When Percival went to get a drink
The water was solid like a skating rink
He bumped his snout on the cold, hard ice
And jumped back in alarm saying, 'That's not nice.'

Diana Blench

Breaking Away

In my dreams I had visions
Of a man making all my decisions.

In my life I had confusion
It was my man showing his illusions.

Having said that, I am now free
With my children wanting to be,
With a future I can now retrieve.

Laura Jennings

Ode To A Surreptitious Love

O'er many years my soul has yearned, by night it's burned,
                              twistèd and turned,
Ne'er ceasing once for all I've earned; in all I seek to find my peace.
It screams aloud a hallowed shriek, through rain and shine, the fine,
                              the bleak;
A call for which my tongue grows weak, yet ne'er will it hasten
                              to cease.

And what, is asked, might it behold? Why, a damsel fair as finest gold,
My treasured queen - a soul unsold - an arcane memory from
                              my youth;
The secret that I'd never tell, a lie that's dragged me clear through Hell,
And that, I fear, is just as well, for even she knew not that truth.

'Twas her whose name in sleep I spoke, and wake would I when
                              sweat a-broke,
For who had heard among my folk the rambled musings of my heart?
The words I ne'er could find to speak, for when I tried my tongue
                              grew weak,
And even now I pray and seek to remedy when she did part.

In dying, 'tis my only thirst, and with that thought I swear I'm cursed;
For all my life I'm better versed in how with her my heart did sway.
Still I weep that she ne'er could know upon me what she did bestow,
And what - in truth - I would forego so she might live another day.

David Maidment

I Talk To God Each Morning

I talk to God every morning
    At the start of each new day
To ask for strength to carry on
    To see me through the fray.

All of our lives we have problems
    For which we are thankful for prayer
Putting our trust in God above
    We need to know He is there.

When life has lost its meaning
    When we come to the end; and it shows
Aimlessly wandering on through life
    Regardless of where the trail goes.

The trail seems to be never-ending
    With sightless eyes staring ahead
We pass from today to tomorrow
    Mentally we're already dead.

Seeking for some comprehension
    Talking to God every day
To ask for strength to carry on
    To see me through the day.

David Livingstone

Thing

It sits on her bed in a coat of brown fur
And each time I see it, it reminds me of her
She was so young when she was taken away
But I know that I'll see her again one fine day

Wherever she went it was always in tow
This wonderful thing she didn't like to let go
It was always her favourite, always there by her side
It was still in her grasp on the day that she died

Her eyes always lit up each time that she saw
This thing that she loved each day more and more
But I didn't know she was out on her own
Or that her favourite thing over the gate she had thrown

But then I heard something that just froze my blood
A squeal of brakes and then a dull thud
I don't know how she opened the gate
By the time that I got there I was seconds too late

For almost four years I kept her in sight
I watched over her each day and each night
Yet the first time I happened to just glance away
Death came and took her on that fateful day

Now she has gone to Heaven above
And there the angels will give her all their love
And I'm so full of sorrow deep down inside
On that fateful day I wish it was me that had died

Donald Linnett

Square Peg In A Round Hole

If all of life were but a dream
Of all the places been and seen
To see our memories good and bad
Some were happy, some were sad.

Why and when and who and what
Did you ever lose the plot?
Was your chin upon your chest?
Even though you tried your best.

Many a tear you may have shed
Lying still within your bed
Hanging on to dwindling hope
Knowing that you had to cope.

To all in life there is a way
If prepared your part to play
Keep the faith, don't let it go
Find your spirit, let it grow.

Paul Lawrence

Capital Punishment

Capital punishment
Should they bring it back
Or should they not?
Violent crimes, murder crimes,
Yes, maybe it should
But what? Hanging or electric chair?
Serious crimes, murder
Violent crimes, serious assault
Found guilty beyond doubt? Yes
If there's any doubt, no
A death row until proven guilty
Capital punishment
Maybe it would help ease crimes
At least they couldn't do it again
Capital punishment
Maybe it should be back

Michelle Knight

The Kiss

He kissed me in the morning
Without any warning.
He kissed me in the afternoon
A trifle too soon.
He kissed me in the evening
When he was leaving.
He kissed me at dawn
When I was about to yawn;
But, he kissed me last night
And it tasted just right.

C A Keohane

Lucky

One day to school assembly I went in orange socks
I took refuge in the corner behind the vaulting box.
The ceremony began with a hymn to Him above
Followed by a sermon, relayed by Mr Dove.

When he had finished preaching he chose to announce
School rules are being broken, on breakers he would pounce!
The theme of his first spot checks, would be to inspect socks -
And those who weren't complying would soon be breaking rocks.

Now at our school the ruling was - 'Socks must be black or grey'
So it looked like I was certain to cop it for that day.
I walked quaking from the corner, dreading my detection
And taking my place in the line queued up for inspection.

'You boy, lift up your trouser legs!' the dreaded master boomed
The chap up front was grinning, his ankles neatly loomed.
By the time it came to my turn, not one boy had been caught!
I'm sure to get my arse striped, my overriding thought.

That day we had the painters in to brighten up the hall
And from a platform overhead a tin began to fall.
It crashed down right in front of me, splattering down,
Polka-dotting Mr Dove, ruining his best gown.

He eyed me up in mock concern and said, 'Boy don't you look quaint,
You're lucky that you only stand knee-deep in orange paint!'

D Kempthorne

Wear A Frown Upside Down And Smile A Mile Wide

It's easy to kneel down and pray,
When you've got something you need to say.
But it's easier to keep your secrets safe,
From day to day.

It's easy to feel you're on top of the world,
When you're being adored.
But it's easier to feel the drop from the fall,
When you're being ignored.

It's easy to speak when you're not afraid,
Of what you might say.
But it's easier to lie, when everyone else
Does exactly the same.

It's easy to smile, when you bite on your teeth,
But to get to the root, you've got to dig deep.
It's easy to smile when you hide what's beneath,
It would take bleach to reach my underneath.
My thing is wrapped up in what I've wrapped it in.
My thing is still wrapped in polythene.
My skin is wrapped up in cellophane,
And my smile is warped, from the hell within.

I wear my frown upside down and smile, a mile wide.

P J Kemp

Sweet Sara May

In youth, she ran the swiftest race
Her fair complexion framed by nut brown curls of texture fine
And large myopic eyes and full red lips adorned a roundly
                                                        featured face
Sweet Sara May.

With music in her heart and every step she walked on air
She sang the sweetest song and deftly fingered tunes from
                                                        all the scores
She played the wedding march, accompanying the choir
Through all those early years, until the day
When she, herself, would walk the aisle
Sweet Sara May.

She milked the Friesian cows and fed their little calves
She gave a hand to sow the seed
To hoe the roots and in the summertime
She loaded bales of hay to fill the barn and family to feed.
Sweet Sara May.

Apple pie and sumptuous fare on Thursdays she would bake
She cooked the grandest meal and
With an icing bag, she weaved and lattice-meshed to decorate
A brother's birthday cake.
Sweet Sara May.

The sheets and shirts and sundry garments all
First to launder, then to press
She liked to knit, to crochet and to tat
And fabricate and stitch the finest dress
Until she donned her wedding veil one day
And so, began her role as Mister Michael's wife.
Sweet Sara May.

Elizabeth Love

Today Is A Gift

Today is new, it's given to me and to you.
It's unblemished shining, gently covered with dew.
If our feet touch it will we spoil or taint?
Will our hands make ugly marks where sun shines faint?
Perhaps our voices or shouting will penetrate the peace.
When things mechanical start, the silence then will cease.

The day moves forward, we prepare and get involved
In daily tasks, essential work, as the hours unfold.
The newness of the morning shades over and we tire.
Noise, bustle, tension, aspirations reaching higher!
All too soon those first quiet thoughts and prayers
Seem to get forgotten, swallowed up with our cares.

Thank You Lord, for refreshing sleep, before tomorrow's dawn.
May we arise rejoicing, see another new day born!
Each morning that appears, Your mercies to us are new,
Fresh hope, new start, a day when we can trust You!
If fearful to know God's healing calm, and not alarm,
Hold us up in your arms. Keep us from all that would harm.

Beryl Lenihan

Promise Or Be Damned!

Red rag to raged bull

And so it continues
We will help, so count the blues . . .
Rely on us . . .
Your support is needed . . .
Expect this or that . . .
Never be in doubt . . .
Who to believe?

If power corrupts - 'peas in pod' left quiescent?
Sprouting forward all directions, but meant
To end in decorum or platitude
Seems not amiss at the time. A feud

History? Merely a phase,
Always truth through time to see - *a daze!*

Truth rests in historical climb
But you can fool some of us all the time!

N Lemel

White Stick

(Taken from the recollections of Albert 'Smiler' Marshall, who served in the 1/1st Essex Yeomanry 1914/1918)

Flanders, nineteen seventeen,
Suddenly our ranks were swelled,
With the arrival of the
Ox and Bucks Light Infantry,
They lifted our spirits somewhat,
In their smart uniforms,
And endless banter and leg pulling,
At six-thirty sharp,
They were ordered over the top,
Going without a fear or care,
With a minimum of fuss,
One called out to me,
'Smiler, keep the kettle boiling,
Soon we'll be back, all of us.'
But by nine all were dead,
Not one survived,
Not one stole another breath,
Several of us went out into
No-man's-land to bury them,
Under the command of an officer of the
Royal Army Medical Corps,
Who waved a white stick in the air,
The Germans acknowledged our task,
I still remember vividly their twisted faces,
So young, so clean, so brave,
Unlived lives, unfulfilled dreams,
We buried three hundred,
As best we could,
Saying a little prayer for each,
Hoping in some way their souls to reach.

P J Littlefield

The Miner

The group of men
Enter the cage
Then wheels slowly turn
Carrying the workers
Down to the bowels of the Earth
To start their day's work
Bogies transport them further along
Miles under the sea
Then they are ready to work
Crouched low, some cut coal
While others fill tubs
To be carried along on a conveyor belt
Theirs is a dangerous and dirty job
Gases and fire-damp are a threat
Also cave-ins,
As men are buried alive
Small pay for the job they do.

Alice Higham

Paradise - By Gaslight

Idiocy is common
Love a fool's paradise
How nice
Idiosyncratic valentine
Cuddle up - double up
Two-time
Idolatrous silken flower
Bloom - overpower
Superabundant recumbent
A cognitive consumption
Surrealistic treat
So nice
Idiocy in paradise.

G Knapton

A Prayer

Our Heavenly Father we ask You today,
To let us be quiet, please help us to pray.
Teach us to be thankful for the life You give,
For Your unselfish love, for the joy to live.
How privileged we are just to be here,
To sit in Your presence knowing You are near.
Please touch our hearts with Your loving word,
Make us humble, we ask You, Lord.
We ask You Father, please bless our home,
For in it, Lord, dwells one of Your own.
Our worries and pain, we give to You,
Let Your healing hands please make us new.
In gladness, Father, we will depart,
Knowing that You, Lord, will stay in our hearts.

Marie Knott

The Train, A View

From the train window
Yellow fields look peaceful despite their violent name.
Green fields lost if they are built on,
Brown fields regained.
A gasometer held up by nothing,
A scarecrow, a straw smile, some kind of lesson?
Now an industrial estate - the fifth - not light,
A suburb without a centre,
An analogy? Of what?
There a warehouse primed to sell me merchandise
I don't know I need yet.
A competition, a view of the world
Pylons, trees, both, none?

John F King

Lonely

Glancing from my window, one bright sunny day
Wishing for someone to share, and be gay
When out from the hedgerow, two little eyes peeped
And from the tall grass, came four little feet.

A pert little hedgehog had come to say
'Please don't be lonely, I've come to play'
Such a nice little fellow, with caring eyes
Seemed to know, he would be a welcome surprise.

No need to be lonely, always someone cares
His small friends and the birds in the air
Be glad to be able to hear, and see
An example to all, who are lonely like me.

C King

God With Us

In the starlit firmament
Shines a beacon star
Coming as a witness
To mankind afar.

Signalling to all men,
A messenger divine
And born this sacred day
Which was the very sign.

No pomp or splendour present
But human in an inn
Born as the Saviour of mankind
And freeing us from sin.

Reg James

The Ash Tree

Hubby and I live in the country,
And close by grows this ash tree
It's always last its leaves to gain,
Then last to take them off again.
I love it most when it is bare,
And often stop and stand and stare.
Paintbrushes I wish I'd had
Or even a pencil and notepad.
Then I could paint or draw this tree
That's growing there for you and me.
I hope that no one will pull it down
Leaving just soil, all earthy and brown.
A motorway we will have soon,
I pray that they will leave some room,
And leave it there to grow and spread
Even after I am dead.

Ann Iverson

The Best Thing In Life Is Laughter

The best thing in life is laughter,
lifts the spirit of oneself.
It's free to all regardless,
of your stature or your wealth.
It's always good to giggle,
have a holler, split one's sides.
And the grumpiest of people,
have potential to grin wide.

Laughter appears from nowhere.
A reaction in the least.
You can stifle to your heart's content,
but you can't control the beast!
Met with open arms at most times,
shared by everyone around.
'Tis the bestest thing to bring a smile
with a wide contrast of sound.

Understood in any language.
Heard or seen by deaf or blind.
So contagious just by being.
I can't help but be inclined.
So be laughter mine eternal.
And for all a welcome guest.
Soothe and ease the stress and strains of life.
Hail laughter be the best!

C J Ireson

Al And Nic

Well, it all started when you were young
First it was Nic, you were ten years old
Then 'Big Al' came on the scene
He caught you in your early teens
This partnership went on for years
You felt like one of 'The Three Musketeers'
All for one and one for all
With Al and Nic you were standing tall

Through endless smoky clubs and bars
Inside - your body bears the scars
Looking through red bleary eyes
You thought there wasn't a better life
And every landlady clapped their hands
Some cartwheeled and did handstands
Yes, you were such a popular guy
Al and Nic brought a permanent 'high'

But now it's hard to breathe and hard to talk
You can't go out cos you can't walk
You can't believe that you've been ditched
But Al and Nic, they wrote the script
In your grubby bedsit, you're all alone,
Al and Nic own you - body and soul . . .

Frank Howarth-Hynes

Battle Not Yet Won

I tried to let you fly and be no more
I tried to scrape myself up from the floor
but every time I'm sure that you have flown
you hit me like a sudden vicious stone

You sting beyond belief, you hold me down
I wish I could replace you with a frown
but never have I been so self-assured
you are unbeaten by the pen and sword.

Cherry Hullock

Wasps

Can I ask please
I know we need bees
But wasps
What was the idea?
Their sting is ferocious
They're very precocious
People panic whenever they're near
The buzz is enough
To put anyone off
And you're told,
'Don't touch them my dear,
If you leave them alone
They will soon fly away.'
Tell that to them
When they're here
They land on your skin
And drill the sting in
The pain is complete agony
They have no particular person in mind
Except they seem to choose *me*
I've had stings on my nose
Even got through my clothes
Never let you know
When they're there
Got stung on my leg
And even my head
The blighters got into my hair
So now when I'm hearing
The buzzing is nearing
I don't panic, I don't run and hide
I get out my spray and give them a blast
When they're dead I put them outside.

J F Hyde

A Dedication

Some friends fear their fathers,
Dads and daughters who'll never speak,
Families torn apart by aggression,
Seeing those tears leaves you weak.

Our family is no longer together,
Thousands of miles leave us to drift,
Your children left with just their mother,
But your love for us, still a gift.

Despite being forever apart,
You're the only man I adore,
The only direction I wish to turn,
The open arms I'll always look for.

Dad, you are my inspiration,
And I understand you being away,
But each day that goes by I long for,
That time when you'll be home to stay.

Sarah Hutchinson

A Joy To Know Thyself

Never seen you look so bright, yet the beauty inside is smiling at me,
like the beauty of moonlight - gently condoling and loving me, keeping
my spirits up and reviving me. I hardly knew but I understand
the way you make me feel. You crushed my pride. No longer hiding
inside - When all I knew was low self-esteem, you taught me how to
love myself. How can I want to be apart, become worried, troubled
and filled with woe? You came and rescued me when I was beside
myself after all had ceased to care - finding love cold as ice but not as
nice - all the pain and heartache you shared, disentangling the bed of
lies. Now I'm happy to know what's inside of me, living and giving of
my best. A precious pearl was found in a field so I went and bought the
field. Now I feel mighty real knowing that I can soar,
like a butterfly, on the winds of love, with God standing by.
Now I'm like a vegetable patch and you're fertiliser which is
sprinkled over me so I can grow. True it be, 'bachelor boy' I may be,
but you came and set me free.

C Marshall-Howell

My Best Friend's Gone

I am sad and feeling lonely, my life is not the same
I lost my best friend recently, a love I won't regain
He was my dog called Spikey; I loved him at first sight
Rescued from a dog home, on impulse on that night

His breed of dog was beagle, sandy, white and beige
That little face touched my heart, while shut up in his cage
Straight away his tail wagged, he jumped all over me
From that moment onward, my heart just jumped with glee

I brought him back to his new home, he settled straightaway
Loving, content and gentle, I can't believe he'd been a stray
I gave him endless loving, took him out for walks each day
Constantly I worried, in case he ran away

Over the three years I had him, he made my life complete
Greeted me when I returned home, sat proudly by my feet
He soon learned how to have a game with dogs over the field
I can't believe how strong our friendship grew, plus trust that
seemed to build

Other people loved him too; he captured all their hearts
So when he suddenly passed away, it tore my heart apart
It's only been a few weeks; will it get easier in time?
Although I try hard to go on, it's hard still not to pine

I constantly keep thinking, *it's now time for his walk*
Tuned in to his dinnertime, to him I'd always talk
When I felt sad and lonely, he was always there
Made things seem worthwhile again, when I felt I didn't care

I will always treasure all these memories, as they will never go
The grief I carry with me, no one will ever know
So rest in peace, dear Spikey, you will never be forgot
You being part of my life, to me means such a lot.

Jayne Hosmer

She's Not What They Think

You'll find her in most bar rooms or clubs around town.
Joking and laughing and acting the clown.
Her eyes are full of sparkle, on her lips a ready smile,
But she isn't showing the tears in her painted eyes.
She's one of life's lonely people who wants a friendly place.
She's not playing 'hard to get', she needs a kindly face.
Life's treated her so badly and she is afraid to try,
Scared to open up her heart and true love passes her by.
Some women get afraid when their menfolk talk to her,
But they should try to get to know this frightened young girl,
'She's only out for one thing' is what they put around,
But, ladies, she doesn't need your man, that's what dragged
                                                        her down.
And, fellas, when you meet her and offer her a drink,
She's not there for you to take, it's just not what you think.
She's just very lonely and needs to talk awhile,
If you really care to look beyond her lonely smile.

Margaret Hooton

Beneath Amber Skies

Longshoreman with the weary eyes
Once full of anecdotes
Beneath amber skies.
Tintinnabulation
A marriage from yesteryear
Gulls fight for scraps
From the alehouse a cheer.
Now so fuddy-duddy
Autumn takes its toll
Low pressure approaching
He's become the role.
The flakes will soon multiply
And I shudder to think
How he'll keep himself strong
I worry, I sink.
Without his dear, dear wife
And his children for company
Just the shipping forecast
In his old hut by the sea.

John Hobbs

Italy - **Memories Of A Camping Holiday, 1952**

The road from Milan to Genoa
stretches endlessly
bordered on each side
by paddy fields,
vast acres of waterlogged vegetation,
nowhere to park a tent.

At sundown we turn off
along a cart track
ending in a farmyard.
'Yes,' we can pitch our tent
on the green square in the courtyard.
Later they invite us
for glasses of wine
and a tour round their garden.
Communication is by hand signs
and the use of a small dictionary.
Oh, the sing-song sounds in Italiano,
how hard 'il suona Inglese'
Cipolla, carota for onions and carrots!

Midnight, we hear the rain
pattering onto the canvas.
We watch with dismay
a puddle forming in the roof above.
Fearing a collapse
Michael climbs out
to tighten the guy ropes
and falls in the channel
bordering the courtyard.

Two o'clock,
the frogs are rejoicing,
croaking their throaty chuckles.
Four o'clock
the Italian farm workers arrive,
they laugh, sing and chatter,
the cows moo and moan
restless in their stalls.

Six o'clock,
we drag ourselves up
and breakfast on
home-baked crusty loaves
and milk straight from the cow.

Time to leave.
We are bidden to a garden seat
to receive gifts from the family,
milk, eggs and cheese,
lettuce, tomatoes, spring onions.
We take photographs
promising to send them.

We wave goodbye
to a place we shall never forget.

Beryl Johnson

Ownership

How is it the light
pours into my temple
for a grand tour of
all the works you have done?

Symmetry and texture form
all set,
the brutish storm elements
elevate my awareness
to where I have become
a foreign trading station.

'No man is an island',
political or other,
the factions that
make my spirit, like valuable
possessions there is ownership.

On recollecting a memory,
Man was creating his science
yet I felt I was surrounded by it
for mine is called Conscience.

Jeremy Jones

For You

M um,
O ver forty years you've raised us, through
T eething, tantrums and teenage hormones.
H elping us to become who we are,
E ncouraging us to be ourselves, to
R each our potential and become
 I ndividual;
N ever leading our lives for us, but
G uiding us in the right direction.

S o this is my time to
U nashamedly, universally and
N aturally
D eclare, that I have always
A dmired you and will never stop loving
Y ou.

Rebecca Johnson

All Soldiers Die

Many boys depart, some will return as men
Leaving loved ones behind, will they see them again?

Ringing church bells plead to win the war
New times await . . . with baggage

If home will not change why will it never be the same?

Returning tidings tell of deaths
Erect monuments, mourn and move on, another life gone . . . in duty

Loyal dogs are often harmed retrieving sticks for their masters

After dancing with the silent lady in battle
She grants your dream to leave, and go home - only in body, as
You are not really there; you are not alone
Living in a nightmare - you left the ballroom with her

The walking wounded leave for home but cadaver incarnations arrive
Swarming crowds gather, beginning searches for survivors

Rejoicing music heard by soldiers as their final elegy, declared
by destiny

Vainly trying to forget etched experiences and disturbing grievances
Haunting terrors playing on private screens

Heroic soldiers gaining posthumous promotion
Providing poor consolation for distraught broken families, living
terrible tragedies

Premature endings seem to create longer remembrances
Diners do not forget the guest who left early

Survivors enduring aftermath, owning still-smoking guns and
bloodstained knives
Seeping scary scenes crowd contorted memories:
Some preferably missing in action than undergoing impossible
reintegration
For scars stay - and each horror show looks back, in flashes

Tantalised and severely shaken, a usual life forcefully forsaken
Nothing can again be the same: no compensation for
inhumane pain

Emotionless faces face grim futures, whilst
Howling animals threaten your stroll - few caring individuals
obstruct your goal

All soldiers die, all soldiers die, all lovers lie, all soldiers die.

Colin Jones

The Sign Reads . . .

'It is an offence . . .
to throw your poetic stones
at this notice . . .
by order of yesterday'.

So do the pick-sniffers rampage:
by-lawing their defence
against sieges.

I threw a brick at it,
when no one was looking.
And you . . . will you blaspheme
against the blasphemy of those words?
Will you cut down this monstrous assassin
with a glinting axe?
But if you do
will you replace it with your own sign?

Perhaps it is better
to suck the sign, like a lolly,
until it melts, smooth and rounded;
imperceptibly.

Peter Jones

Jesus Christ

Footsteps fall in cold winter frost,
Raindrops fall and then they're lost,
Kingdoms fail, in the blink of an eye, up and die.

'What could last forever?' I hear you ask,
'And what eternal love could keep us together?'
'The love of God!' I quickly reply,
'The love of God?' they ask as they sigh,
'But why? Oh why? And what does that imply?'

'It's above us all, it's beyond our understanding,' I say,
'It's like the seasons and the stars, like the waves,
And the birds and the bees,
It's like a cool summer breeze, like the winter snow.'

'Yes, but how the hell do you know?'
'How the hell do I know? I'll tell you how . . .

God is in people and everyone loves and needs people,
It's just that we can't see Him, I believe,
It seems to me that He is in everyone's heart,
He is in everyone's foreground, middle distance and background,
And what beats me is that He loves effortlessly, gracefully
                                        and wonderfully,

His Name *is* Jesus Christ . . .'

Simon P Jones

My Friend

The shining youth dissolved, in irksome confinement,
Within the rooms of the office, for six and thirty years,
Content as a caged animal, I became part of my desk,
A wooden soul and pending work, I forgot how to smile,
Sundays were mine with gloomy weight, hanging in the air,
Shopping, washing and cleaning, and going to church,
The first flutter of holiday, a glittering phantom stirred,
To air myself in fields and parks, with my best friend.
Alas! My doctor warned me to halt, cancer held me down,
The deadly grip of the poisonous snake swallowed my fantasies.
I lay in a corner of my house, without looking at a watch,
The day of the week, or of the month, was meaningless to me,
Then he came to me, like sunshine, with a basket full of love,
'My beloved friend,' said he to me, his smile was life-giving,
'Can you live one single day with that creative spark in you,
To pen your best work yet to come, in the bliss of solitude?
Live your life while life is there as life is beautiful,
Life and death are well distanced, your journey incomplete.'
He was to me a cool breeze, and he took me for walks,
Old jokes we cracked together, through the countryside lovely,
He did my laundry while I slept, and all my shopping too,
Read my favourite author to me at my bedside dismal,
When treatment made me raw with pain his love imparted life,
I lived through it holding his hands and emerged triumphantly,
Oh! My guardian angel friend I owe my life to you.

P K Janaky

The Dawning Of A New Day

In the still summer morning

A new day was dawning
Blackbird sang his morning song
Soon other birds joined along
The sound of their music filled the air
No other sound could compare.

Frogs on the lily pond awoke
Along with a toad they began to croak
An owl caught out late returned to the barn
'Tu-whit tu-whoo,' said he as he reached the farm.

The cockerel crowed his awakening call
To the cat sleeping peacefully on the wall
She stretched her limbs and began to scratch
Whilst thinking about all the vermin she'd catch

Far down in the sleepy valley
In the meadow so verdantly green
A dairy cow bellowed loudly
To a sheepdog which she had seen

Sheep on the hillside stirred from their grazing
At all the noise which they found quite amazing
The valleys and hills were alive that morn
Another new day had just been born.

Christine Hardemon

The Songster

There was a lady named Mrs MacVeen
Whose canary would only sing 'God Save the Queen',
It sang it by night and it sang it by day
In spite of what Mrs MacVeen would say,
'Little Bo-Peep' would be nice to hear
Or 'Rock-a-bye Baby' would pleasure the ear,
Chirp about winter or chirp about spring
But do stop chirping that same darn thing.'

But the bird only stared at Mrs MacVeen
And went on with its singing of 'God Save the Queen',
So she finally gave the canary away
To a loyalist neighbour, Mrs MacVay,
Who fed the bird with expensive seed
That gave its feathers a glorious sheen
And by day and by night she heard with delight
Its rendering of 'God Save the Queen'!

Margaret Rose Harris

Friends

Where are they now, those pals of yesterday,
Whose bright young faces shone at early morn,
Whose happy laughter stretched beyond the dawn.
Who at that time the world held in their hand,
As is the case with youth in any land.

Where are they now, those pals we loved so well?
Perhaps ours is not to know,
And theirs is not to tell.
One thing we'll learn; a never-ending truth;
Old age can never quite recapture,
The wild intoxicating,
Never to be forgotten,
Long-lost friends of youth.

Windsor Hopkins

Summer Days

The calm of those summer days,
With an early morning haze,
Which predicts hot weather,
Which we take for good measure.
The flowers blossoming,
Gardeners cosseting,
The diamond-shaped petals,
The brilliant colours settle
On the beauty of summer days,
With love we direct our gaze.

I T Hoggan

The Break

Brief lines,
hastily erased
from a foreign postcard.
Confession,
scrapped and scattered
over a foreign beach.

A bad idea,
rubbed out
and blown away.
She flew out the next day.

Now the thin,
sun-dead skin
that lay with him
on that foreign beach,
showers
like those thin bits
of graphite and rubber.

With every soft stroke of her towel,
it confetties onto her
chequered English bathmat,
and what clings,
is quickly concealed
beneath thicker,
more sensible layers,
and left to shrivel in private.

Then she leaves the bathroom,
which for the first time in her married life,
she realises
has been locked.

John Kay

Tuna

Tuna flashing through the ocean
chasing prey down with devotion
Atop the chain
it flies the main
till nylon halts its headlong strain

A billion years of evolution
still no time to find solution
Only aim a meal to get
first, and last time, in a net,
conveyor belt to High Barnet.

Trolley trundles through the store
stops at sign marked 'Albacore'.
Magnificent fish sans skin and fin
still in brine, now in a tin.
Must press on, I'm feeling thin.

A tear-soaked eye, I have a peep,
for this colossus of the deep.
A pause at meal to meditate
this king of fish now on my plate.
Whose only sin, to taste so great.

Derek B Hewertson

Sweet Music

Music is my life and soul
It fills my heart with gladness
Every day it keeps me whole
And drives away my sadness

Music turns a winter's day into a breath of spring
The north wind whistles as it blows
Just listen to the skylark sing
Or rippling water as it flows

Music makes me want to dance
Tuneful airs fill my head
Like waltzes, foxtrots, lancers,
Quicksteps, sambas, goodness knows
I will take my chances.

Music finds a way
(Although we may not know it)
It fosters thought and keeps us calm
Or urges us to blow it

Then somehow when we sing
On karaoke in the pub
Trying to sing like Frank or Bing
On bath night in the tub
To keep in tune is another thing
And blimey, there's the rub!

So all you music lovers
As you struggle with a tune
With lyrics like the moon and June
And words of love divine
I say to you, 'Don't bother
Unless you have a voice like mine.'

J W Hewing

Your Guiding Light

(Kyrielle)

When I was lost on the path of life,
How heavy pressures caused me strife
Once I saw I knew it right,
My Lord, I saw Your guiding light:

This guiding light I seemed to know,
A certain path I had to go:
Your glow that shines so really bright
My Lord, I saw Your guiding light:

To follow in the glow not stray,
Lord, You've shown the perfect way:
Protecting me from trials and plight,
My Lord, I saw Your guiding light:

Caressed by love this light does show,
Live your life for good and know:
Believe in Him and life is bright,
My Lord I saw Your guiding light:

Leave the darkness right behind,
Peace of mind one day will find:
Feel Your strength so full of might,
I have seen Your guiding light.

Betty Hattersley

Remembering You

Remembering you
In a pink haze
Of romance
Loving
Caring
Long summer days

Remembering you
A laugh, a joke
Your touching
Tenderness
Sharing
The cigarette smoke

Remembering you
Without even trying
The wheezing
Coughing
And pain
It's me who's dying.

Geraldine Laker

Home

Long before we reach You,
You run to welcome us,
Like the Prodigal Son's return,
Promising to make a home with us,
An everlasting dwelling place,
Where Your glory is,
Mighty God, source of all joy,
I long to see those many mansions,
Send Your spirit upon us now,
Bind us together,
While Earth is not our home,
We are strangers in this land,
Going to the cross,
You gave up everything for us,
You brought us home at last.

Christine Julian-Huxley

Have A Lemonade

This bus stop is not here; it is *not* in use,
for *bus* times, see the rubber one
chained up next to it, then blow out the fuse.
Imagine my surprise, waking up in a car
to be told that it'd crashed into a TV commercial
on a screen where you are!
Have a lemonade,
have a leap of faith,
be the hybrid of a bolted mare running onto a bull at a gate;
have a fat cigar, boy; have a Patsy Cline voice;
have a stupid moan at yer student loan
and smack yer study wall with yer camera-phone
and wake up holding yer own;
let nothing you dismay,
let none you underrate,
you've just witnessed Des Cartes,
Newton, Mesmer, Freud and Gates
having pigs of a day.

Tom Hathaway

Cat-Sat And In Love

Dear Eileen, great joy is upon me today,
I feel so excited you're coming to stay,
My tail's like a feather, all fluffed up and wide,
I'm feeling so warm and contented inside.

Now you rest, and I'll make us dinner tonight
Prepare you my best culinary delight
I thought maybe prawns and a fish from the sea,
My mate's got a boat, he can fetch them for me.

And after we dine, would you like to step out?
You dance on the clover, I'll shuffle about,
I once used to tap dance but now I'm too fat,
Still, shuffling's enough for an overweight cat.

Not being familiar, oh look, I've gone red!
But I'd deem it an honour to join you in bed,
Well, not inside but outside, right down by your feet,
Not up near your face cos my breath's not too sweet.

Oh Eileen, I love you, you're my shining star,
And as for my owners, let them stay where they are!

Moya Hastings (and Scat!)

An Age-Old Fable

Love had brushed its scarlet wings with breathtaking beauty
Against the cheek of a vulnerable soul; whose dying embers
Fanned by Obsession's lurid sigh, sparked a wondrous journey
Between the newborn seeds of Intuition and Heart's fertile soil.

It came in the night; a soft-footed intruder in disguise
How strange, then, Love recognised him without hesitation
Made quick its voyage to reconcile her smile and her eyes
Shivered upon contact; with burning fever, not bittersweet cold.

Now Longing has awoken from its restful hibernation
Squinting at the blinding light of Desire it finds upon waking
With renewed vigour after so long in hiding, it sings out to her
Like a newborn child from shadowed abyss into radiant glow.

Tonight she awaits Moon's solitary eclipse; Love begs to stay
Yet Parting readies to stride forward and meet her in the dark
In angel's tears she tries in vain to swim for Life's great answer
It eludes and teases - floating away, just of out Comfort's reach.

Love remained planted with solid roots; wings static and clipped
A defenceless spirit still holds them close against her chest
Fire smoking and rekindled by Memory's sweet warm breeze
Her smile kept alive in moments of Imagination's choosing.

Deborah Headspeath

The Shift

I knew the fault
was not my own
the day I left -
leaving half-truths
whole lies
innuendo
and deception -
escaping
into childhood
to search out
whole truths
white lies
trees to hug
flowers to press
air to breathe -
(for he counted my breaths)
seeking proof
that I was not flawed
nor my years wasted -
ran back to Mama
like a babe
to the womb
comforted
by the consistent
beat of her heart
the truth
in her eyes
the salvation
of a locked door
to coax new roots
that would not strangle
a resolve
that would not waver
and so
begin again.

Ethel Kirkpatrick

For My Friend

Whenever I needed someone to cheer me up,
You were there.
Whenever I needed a shoulder to cry on,
You were there.
Whenever I needed a friendly face,
You were there.
Whenever I needed someone to talk to,
You were there.
In the future, when I look for your smile,
You won't be there.
But I'll think of your smile,
And I'll think of our memories.
I'll remember the good times we've had
And know that you'll be happy,
And others will be privileged,
To be your friend,
As I was.

Katie Wood (15)

A Silent Journey

Bit by bit, thoughts scatter, dissolving on a sea of silence.
Years I waited, listening intently, to the never-ending source of me.
Thrust far beyond, the wakening time, to an open place,
of memory not.

Constant, naked, unmoved, unmoving, I hover somewhere,
out of touch, out of time. A wave crashes over, on the summer shore,
I dive, still unknowing, the least trodden path.

Music to my heart astounding, listening with an urgent need, I see a
thought and follow briskly, shedding worries that hinder progress,
agony and ecstasy, in perfect balance, forward moving.

Blank pages fill the void, a symphony of sound, yet there still I hover,
on the edge of my deep abyss. More perfect than myriad thought,
a future history, in far years to be written, if only then
I can reach the end!

Ego less, self, the one and only truly me, I abide my time, in this place
still, journeying a journey far from I. Years seem minutes
as minutes are hours, on the edge of the hovering thought life.
Watching the moments drift by, with a detached curiosity, awaiting
the time to strike, to move with a swift grace, the place set and
appointed for this journeying I.

The door opened and then the door closed, in I leapt with fiery glee.
Now all doors are open except the door that is closed, I cannot
go back, to that one closed-off space. The silence is great, reaching
deep, to the very soul and at last I can turn and say to you, 'I see!'

Michael Skerratt

Knowledge

Watching the soul at play
Through blue windows of sight
World of form upside down
Reversed by controlling mind
Colours collide soul speaks
Forming an eternal body out of vibrating light
Spine tingles with an awakened thought
Disturbing snakes that entwine within the code of life
They listen for the sound of the breathless voice
Calling to journey upon its resonance
Soul light turns within an illusion sigh
Painting Heaven on a smiling forehead
Whirling blood cells compete to sing
Spinning faster and faster they cry out to be heard
Their voices resonate within the heart of the possessor
Destroying the veil that covers the face of the soul
Frozen in a thought of time and space
Man covered in the shroud of indifference
Struggling to rise to touch the vine that hangs above
The stone bed that is slept upon by an enquiring mind
Water flows in torrents upon the sodden floor
Wine runs through veins to satisfy a drunken heart
Soul rests upon an eternal dream.

James Walsh

Things

From some dull slump sleep
I wake up gasping,
Bits of Jesus all over me.
You are
Dried onto the window sills of my mind.

I remember the first evening we met.
Carnaby Street.
Your drunken haunched bounds slinging towards me like a
terrible mistake,
Your out-held hand that was like an earthy Heaney spade
And I didn't see the trail of guts and bloodied hearts you'd made.
At the pub I used words like basically, really and suss,
You used words like Antipodean, libation and thus.
I was captivated by your glance,
By your brain, the size of France
And when you spoke I wanted to climb into your mouth and dance.

Your low and Eton-boom accent sent sharp signals to my brain,
my balls:
Get out of this now, there is too much to compute here,
But I was gripped-still: a sluice gate to the white-water torrents
That were your conversations.
I could see planets in your pockets,
Baudelaire on your fingers and
Political movements lodged in your teeth.
It was all I could do to just nod and smile
While my brain adjusted to these dim explosions.
Months on I am still reeling,
Realising all the things that you are.

You're a stegosaurus, quietly mighty and only yourself, nuzzling
extinct horticulture.
You're an unbridled horse with wise and weary blacks for eyes.
You're a Neanderthal wandering the bracken heath,
A grinning tribesman kicking dirt amid a rainbow of blood
and feathers,
An Oxford squire, sucking the last of the Ale House Tawny Port,
A pirate pacing the black galleons of the Caribbean,
A raucous lord, drunk on his own wealth and filled with
roasted partridge.

You're all these things
And a hundred more.
From some dull slump sleep
I wake up gasping.

I can't get you out of my mind.

Patrick Farrelly

Alone With My Fears

Wave after wave they find harbour, restless;
Always asking questions that have no answers.
The more I dive into the dark mire of this sea,
I am crushed by despair of all this futility.

My feelings have words but are unable to speak
Because of the fears that cause havoc and wreak
Not. Dumb. Numb. If only people knew how I felt
Often I prayed and often I knelt.

I live in the hope that all will be well with me,
That I shall stop being crushed against this wall
Of insanity, with its constant wave of Dead Sea
Scrolling, that Light will shine through the squall

Life goes on around me, life goes on inside of me
One is seen, the other invisible; if only they knew
If only they could see, what would they do for me?
If anything at all, they would spew, they would spew.

I am left alone with my fears of yesterday and its
Angry path that forges deeper into the deep
Hidden where no one can find or enter its
Emotional cavernous sorrow. Imprisoned keep.

Even so am I blessed. Emmanuel. *Amen.*

E J Clark

The Street Lamp

The street lamp and its flicker
Beating like a pulse
Holds no perch for birds
But stutters through the lonely night
Only glimpsing the movements in the dark
And, blind it may be in the daytime
But when its heart thumps
It holds a view
Of all the street around it
Empty and melancholy
And crying the tears of gunshots
As they echo through an empty darkness
Far in the streets ahead
The street lamp beats its customary pulse
And gives the street a heart and life
But when the sun arises from its frosty slumber
The street lamp loses its stuttering beam
The bulb is replaced with a new one
And it shines throughout the night
It holds no character and gives no life
And all who are near, avoid its gaze
As they keep into the darkness,
So their secrets can be safe
Until they can find another
Beating street lamp, like the one they knew so well.

Callan J Davies

Clouded Hourglass

Oh the unexpected!
Sudden ruptured smite!
Open-barrelled ending to a
Light beyond warm gloom.
Carried forward blatantly,
Rocked unconscious angrily and
Plucked before a towering guard the
Troubles of our grasping hands.

Walking long uncharted,
Milked beneath the moon;
Dragging limp the parodies of
Ancient thumping fools.
Connecting with the shimmering
A willow in the puddle's stare
An invite to a crushing room waits
Our fate of mourning hesitance.

Looking round hysterical!
Incessant under grief;
Clutched the bleeding hyacinth
Whilst running from our view.
The quivering bells tolled apathy
Of shaking pouring symmetry yet
On this trail of righteousness we still
Bellow out our faked regrets . . .

Daniel Heath

Faithful

The grandeur echoed through hastily written notes,
Destined for the sands that time takes away,
Earthen desire speaks through the space inside,
Freedom wanes in the distance,
Leave others' greed fresh,
Dream.

Jordan van't Hof

Coping With Cancer

I feel so very lonely; it's the loneliness of the misunderstood,
No one, not one person knows what's going on in my head.
I have trouble making sense of the whirling thoughts myself.
One minute they are spinning out of control at dizzying speeds,
The next . . . nothing. My mind is blank. A void of nothingness.

I have moments of great, unexplained happiness enveloping me,
I can do anything! If I can deal with this I can take on the world
Then the next minute, my heart, my soul, plummet to
unknown depths.
How can I cope with this? The darkness, the fear, the uncertainty
of it all?
The world whizzes past me as I sit stock-still, not knowing, not caring.

Then he takes my hand, my soulmate, my rock is beside me now.
His warm, strong hand stroking the back of my neck. Comforting,
loving,
Then there's another warm hand, a tiny hand, sticky from
strawberry jam,
Wiping away my tears, smiling and demanding that Mummy
tickle her.
Then I know I can do this, we can fight this together, for as long
as it takes.

Michelle Borrett

Words Unspoken

I wanted to tell you,
How sorry I was,
For the way things turned out
But somehow, I never did,
And now it seems wrong,
To bring up the past.

Some day, it will be too late,
And I'll never have told you,
How sorry I am.

Beverley Ann Rudd

Point Of Life

Existence
For animals, birds, mammals
Is but a dance
Of mortality

Why die every day
Of existence?
Why imitate wildlife
When we can live civilised
With a good chance
Of immortality

To continue breathing
Even after death
Assassinate
Heavy breaths of anger
Hot sighs of envy
Lewd gasps of desire
Crude yawns of emptiness
To get lightened
To become a citizen
Enlightened.

S M Sivaraman

Sophia's Poem

W ildlife springs
O ak trees sway
O ld twigs on the floor
D affodils sprouting everywhere
L ife is simple, life is pure
A nimals hibernate once a year
N aughty squirrels playing with nuts
D aybreak dawns again.

Danielle Wills (13)

The End

Rings of love, circles of water
Can't stop thinking about her
Walls too tough, eager to break them down
Fallen trees, made a happy girl sad
Promises broken, shattered dreams
Did I really mean nothing?
Reaching hands, drifting away
Echoing thoughts, why, why, why?
The pain just wanders, a voodoo doll
The pin is in your eyes
Hatred beckons, barriers raised
Night falls, the days have gone
Voice of reason, whispered sins
The giant has all but fallen
Hearts are broken, gambled lives
Bailiffs on my soul
Trembling voices, memories die
Life has ended, own goal
Door closes, walk of shame
Loneliness sinks in
Pictured tombstone, dying flowers
Fading, going, going, gone.

Dean Squires

Synaesthesia

Calling water colourless
Is like saying there is no music
In a summer afternoon:
No flavour in fear
Or falling in love.
To deny the way the water
Takes and breaks a rainbow
Is to say it is, after all,
Only water.

Richard Hain

Spoil Heap

The world is but a spoil heap
Mere remnants of a more beautiful Earth
Now buried under time
Only shadows of the past.
The green of the fields, harvested.
The blue of the river, drained.
The men merely rocks,
Dependant only upon themselves,
Uncaring.
But amongst the dull uninteresting lives,
There is one that sparkles
And gleams in the darkest hole.
It is a friend.
A friend to treasure always
And bring happiness to a world in need.

Lucy Downes (14)

Day And Night

When the sun finally arrives
he hands out flowers on street corners.

He springs from sprouting bushes,
indiscriminately molesting members of the public.

He forcibly removes the fur coats
from off the backs of old women.

He wears an orange sandwich board
and shimmies up the main street.

He climbs, in his royal naked nudity,
through the high windows of churches.

He licks the gaudy golden belt buckles
on the waists of garish girls, until,

the moon, in a white coat,
with bald head and round rimless glasses,

pulls up in a van, and prowls
behind the torch of himself.

Stephen Brown

Return Of The Boyfriend Snatcher

You're nubile and you've got pert boobs
You're built like a toothpick
You're like whipped cream, as some might say
That's fresh and smooth . . . and thick

You flutter your false eyelashes
And dye your hair to fit
Your latest conquest's heart's desires
. . . A tart's identikit

You've passed exams in perming hair
Well, whoopee bloody do!
You've got a brain, it's just a shame
It lacks a cell or two

You've got your own quaint 2-bed flat
Who needs cheap B&Bs?
You beat me on experience
With sex, and STDs

You don't have female friends, unless
They pose no threat at all
And one or two who'll drive you places
At your beck and call

Those boys they come a'running
Dumping girlfriends left and right
To get into your wayward knickers
Each and every night . . .

. . . You're flexible, it's clear to see
Your legs won't stay together
Monogamy just ain't your thing
And yet you think you're clever

Your ideal man is someone
Who's engaged to someone else
You'd fancy Quasimodo
If he *wasn't* on the shelf

But hey, there's no hard feelings
And I wish you well, it's true
I'm never one to hold a grudge
Cos I've more class than you

And I'll resist the urge to come
And give you a good slap
. . . From knowing you'll end up alone
And riddled with the clap!

Bee Gordan

Pull The Udder One Wit By Half

On my first day on the farm I was filled with much alarm,
When I was asked to milk a cow, because I was not sure how,
Because udders, cows have four; of these this much I was sure,
Well my problem was no fun; I could only find the one.

I just wondered how, to milk this poor disfigured cow,
I found just one teat but upon the breast, I could not find the rest,
I went about my task, you see, ignoring the lack of the other three,
Well, I knew it was a test, and I just had to try my best.

I grasped the uni-udder as I could not find another,
I pulled it with a pace, until the sweat ran down my face,
A herder wandered by and looked me in the eye,
And said, 'I am no vet, but would you like to make a bet?'

'What bet is that?' says me. 'That you get no milk,' says he,
'I am betting that you fail, to get any milk in that pail.'
So I bet him fifty quid, wishing that I never did,
Now I will not stop, until I fill that pail to the top.

I gave it my best try, but my bucket stayed quite dry,
Not a drop of milk could I get, but I am still trying yet,
The herder made his way back in, on his face a mocking grin,
He said after a while, 'I won my wager then,' with a smile.

I paid up on my bet but I wasn't finished, not just yet
With the herder who took my money, thinking it was funny,
'Just how did you know, how, I'd get nothing from that cow?'
He said, 'The cow, you fool, that you've been milking is a *bull!*'

Christopher Ashford

Poetry Now Information

We hope you have enjoyed reading this book - and that you will continue to enjoy it in the coming years.

If you like reading and writing poetry drop us a line, or give us a call, and we'll send you a free information pack.

Alternatively if you would like to order further copies of this book or any of our other titles, then please give us a call or log onto our website at www.forwardpress.co.uk

Poetry Now Information
Remus House
Coltsfoot Drive
Peterborough
PE2 9JX

(01733) 898101